THE TALK

THE TALK

LEADING YOUR CHILDREN INTO THE REST OF THEIR LIVES

RICK THOMAS

THE TALK:
Leading your Children into the Rest of Their Lives

ISBN 978-1-966741-07-7

Rick Thomas

Edited by Sheron Wallace

Life Over Coffee
8595 Pelham Rd Ste 400 #406,
Greenville, SC 29615
LifeOverCoffee.com

Hebrews 13:4
Let marriage be held in honor among all, and let the marriage bed be undefiled, for God will judge the sexually immoral and adulterous.

For additional resources, visit
lifeovercoffee.com

Table of Contents

Preface

This book is not just about the sex talk. Though its content will be a great practical help for you when the time comes to have this all-important conversation with your child, I want to provide you with a long runway that prepares you for the talk. Some readers may want to get to the crux of the talk; I understand. You can't wait because there is no runway; your child is transitioning from youth to young adult, and you must start the talk sooner than later. If that is you, you may skip to the final three chapters to get to the nuts and bolts of the talk.

However, the best use of this book is for the parents of a toddler. The sex talk begins in the early months of a child's life, specifically with how the parents live out biblical sexuality in the home as a couple. Your goal is to do more than export scripted words to your child at the pivotal point as a pre- or early teenager. You are uniquely positioned to give your child a worldview, a lifestyle, and an example of biblical sex in the home, the church, and the world. This book is about parenting one of the most confusing and complicated areas in a child's life. What you're about to read can transform you, your marriage, and your child. It is one of those rare gospel perspectives about a complex subject. Be prepared for God to change you. Be prepared to lead your child into the rest of their life.

NOTE TO READER: This book has several chapters that discuss one gender or the other, which is intentional, so I would not have to say him/her throughout. If you have a girl, everything I say will apply to her, too.

Chapters 1-5 are foundational. They are essential as you lay a foundation for establishing and enhancing your relationship with your spouse and child while interacting within those relationships. Sexuality and the sex talk are not disconnected from the history and patterns of the relationships, which is why this book does not begin with the talk.

Chapters 6-8 walk through the talk. With a relational foundation in place, you are now ready to walk your child through the sex talk. The final three chapters of this book will guide you through this process.

Introduction

The sex talk begins in a child's toddler years as they learn about sexuality, intimacy, and relationships through the attitudes, words, and interactions of their parents. Sex is a shame-laced subject because of our mutual fallenness. One talk just before they head off to their next school grade is not enough to help them think right about gender, identity, and sexuality. Even our worldly counterparts—though they give the appearance of no sex shame and have all the answers—are not free from sexual entanglements.

Sexual Confusion

Then the eyes of both were opened, and they knew that they were naked. And they sewed fig leaves together and made themselves loincloths.

(Genesis 3:7)

It is our collective ignorance and embarrassment with sex that motivate us to keep sexual communication tucked behind our Adamic fig leaves, which is precisely why biblical parents want to model and practice biblical sexuality in the home. Sexual communication (koinonia) begins early in a child's life because sex is not just about the physical act. Our sexuality cannot be pared down to a weekend retreat with a child so the parent can explain the birds and bees to them. Sexuality is an unavoidable, communal, everyday, interactive lifestyle for all people.

Long before there is physical interplay between a man and a woman, there are non-negotiable elements of sex that children need to learn. For example, the physical act of sex should be characterized by the elements of gentleness and kindness. Being kind to another person is a choice that makes physical intimacy the way God intended. You can't do sex right without being kind to the person you're intimate with. Who wants to have sex with an unkind or ungentle person? A caring person will perform sex with the intent of exalting the name of Christ through other-centered love-making. Sexual love is not sexual abuse.

Parental Leadership

The sex of the unkind soul is death by a thousand paper cuts, destroying what physical intimacy should be. Biblical parents want their children to learn an other-centered way of life, which is why they want to model the life of Christ in their homes—at the very beginning of their children's lives. A child's view of sex and sexuality is primarily shaped by their personal observations and interactive experiences in the home. By the time a parent leads their child through the sex talk during the preteen years, the foundation of sexuality has already been laid and inculcated into the child's mind.

Parents have the privilege to create a gospel-saturated sexuality worldview that will make the future sex talk with the child come across as something consistent with the child's experience with the parent's sexuality in the home. In this book, I teach you how to create that runway that leads to the inevitable sex talk. It's a runway that looks like Christ and the church in all the fullness of what a marriage should be, including physical intimacy.

Call to Action

As you think about teaching your child about physical intimacy, the best place to prepare is your heart and lived experience. I trust these self-assessment questions will guide you in such a way that you can teach your child about sex by saying, "Follow me as I follow Christ" (1 Corinthians 11:1).

1. Sex is about kindness. What are your children learning about kindness from your example?
2. Sex is about selflessness. What are your children learning about selflessness from your example?
3. Sex is about maturity. What are your children learning about maturity from your example?
4. Sex is about love. What are your children learning about love from your example?

1

Parenting from Zero to Adulthood

The goal of parenting is to rear a child to adulthood as a man or woman living under God's authority. The hope-filled goal is for your child to step out into God's world that final time, as they exit your home, as a person under His authority. The transition from when they once submitted and obeyed you, now they desire to submit to and obey God as an adult operating as missional agents in His world. This process of training a child to that future aspiration happens in three stages.

Child Development

The first stage is the dependent stage, the second is the interdependent stage, and the final one is the independent stage. The rule-of-thumb breakdown is as follows:

1. The dependent stage is from 0 to 2 years of age.
2. The interdependent stage is from 2 to 22 years of age.
3. The independent stage is from 22 years of age until death.

Each stage is a window of time that flexes depending on

the child, the parents, and the situations that influence a child's maturation through each stage. For example, some children will be independent long before their twenty-second birthday, and others will live with their parents long after that date. The stages are suggestive, not binary. Also, the word independent is used in a limited sense, speaking only to a person's ability to function well in the culture while providing a means for subsistence. Self-reliance is a non-communicable attribute that belongs to God. Not even Jesus was self-reliant (John 5:30). The typical starting time for their limited independence is when a child graduates college, hence the 22-year line for the transition.

Dependent Stage

From birth to the two-year mark, a child is dependent on his parents (or guardians). An infant can do little to take care of himself. Even as early mobility begins, he does not have the mental or physical capacity to live alone. By the time a child is two years old, his ambition to explore the world around him surpasses his mental and physical capacities to keep up with his Adamic aspirations. This combination of limited intelligence and ever-increasing independence converge to create a stage of life some parents call the terrible twos, which is a terrible name. This stage is not terrible, but it is an opportunity for a parent to bring shape to a small soul that knows no bounds and will run as wild as the parent permits.

This age is one of the most amazing times in a child's life. He begins to learn valuable character traits that will shape his heart for the rest of his life. Humility, honor, integrity, submission, obedience, honesty, discretion, love, serving, and self-control are a few of the character seeds that a parent begins to plant into the child's heart. Structure, compliance, and obedience are the most essential things at this early stage. If done well, these seeds will manifest as good fruit in a young person's life. I'm not discounting the grace of God, which transcends all our efforts, but speaking exclusively to the role of a parent to plant and water while trusting God for future growth. A two-year-old's boundless energy and capacity to learn provide the proactive parent with a pliable student for learning in every context and situation in his life.

Interdependent Stage

As the child migrates out of the dependent stage, the parent works at redrawing and expanding the lines of responsibility between what the child should be doing and what the parent should be doing; the child does more and the parent does less. The child's growing capacities enable him to take on new and increasing responsibilities, which he is eager to accept. This line redrawing-expansion process continues to evolve throughout the child's young life. The child is malleable, and the stage is fluid. The parent operates in the Spirit (pneumatically), always adjusting according to progressive changes in the child. The objective is always to shift the responsibilities away from the parents while giving them to the child.

Like a time-released capsule, the parent is incrementally releasing the child into God's world. Nearly all of the heavy parental lifting happens before the child is 12 years old. The teenage years are more about affirming and adjusting the parental work that the parents parented into the child during the previous decade. Like slow-setting cement, the teenage years are when the child becomes mostly set in his ways. His manner of living (Ephesians 4:22) is in place, as he experiences an inward and increasing compulsion to do life independently. When the parent comes to the counselor with a rebellious teen, in almost all cases, it's too late—if the expectation is to change the child at this moment. The cement is set, and it will only be the pressure of God that breaks the young adult's heart, reorienting him to the Lord.

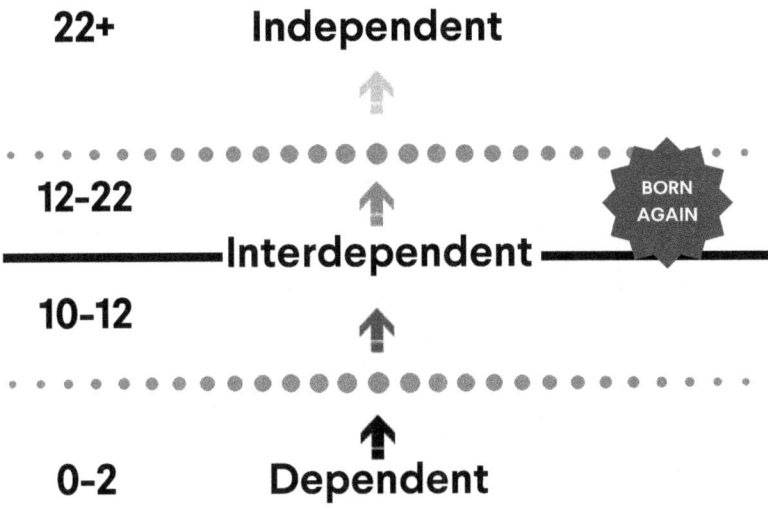

22+   **Independent**

12-22   **Interdependent**   BORN AGAIN

10-12

0-2   **Dependent**

The interdependent years reveal the parent's modeling and teaching during the dependent years. I'm not suggesting that the parents are at fault primarily if they have a rebellious teen, but they will be the primary shaping influences for good or evil.

- The first half of the interdependent stage (2 to 12) is the parent's primary work in the child's heart.
- The last half of the interdependent stage (12 to 22) is when the parent motivates the child to continue as they are or to try to adjust any broken things.

Most of the time, it's a combination of the two. The child is mostly good, and the parent is spurring him on to maturity (Hebrews 10:24-25). Or, the child is mostly disobedient, and the parent is looking for reinforcement through intervention, hoping the child does not walk away from the faith of the parents.

Regeneration

Regeneration is the parent's secret weapon and only hope for the child's transformation (John 3:7; Romans 10:9; Revelation 20:15). Everything else is window dressing, or as Jesus talked about in Matthew 23, it's someone who may look good on the outside, but the inside is rotten to the core. If he is born again at any time during his childhood, the grace of God will transform any bad parental practices or Adamic influences. Redemption is the parent's only genuine safety net. No matter how awful a parent is or how evil the child is, God's grace can gather it all and nail it to the cross of Christ. The birth, life, death, resurrection, ascension, and intercession of Christ can change any child.

The best and worst parents are hopeless outside of God's grace-empowered regeneration of their children. This theological and unbending truth is where good and bad parents—however you determine such things—must guard their hearts. A legalistic parent will think they made their child bad because of their personal failures. A different type of legalistic parent will think they made their child good because of their righteous deeds. Both of them err. It is not about parenting primarily but about the grace of God in a child's life. Parenting can be an asset or a liability—no doubt, but the critical matter is that every parent must anchor their hope in the transformation that God provides, for by grace, a child will turn out well (Ephesians 2:8-10).

Independent Stage

Let's say your child completes college and is back at home, which is not necessarily wrong. There does not have to be any shame in living with your parents. Lucia lived with her parents until she married me when she was 28 years old. She thought about living on her own but chose not to because of several compelling reasons. Lucia had a great relationship with her parents. She had no interest and saw no particular benefit in living on her own. She worked full-time and was fully providing for herself. She gave her parents a modest monthly rent payment as though she was living on her own. She saved her extra money for marriage, praise God. She extended and enjoyed her relationship with her parents, which she knew would considerably diminish after she set up her autonomous domestic empire with me. She benefited from the best of both worlds: being with her parents while living independently in God's world.

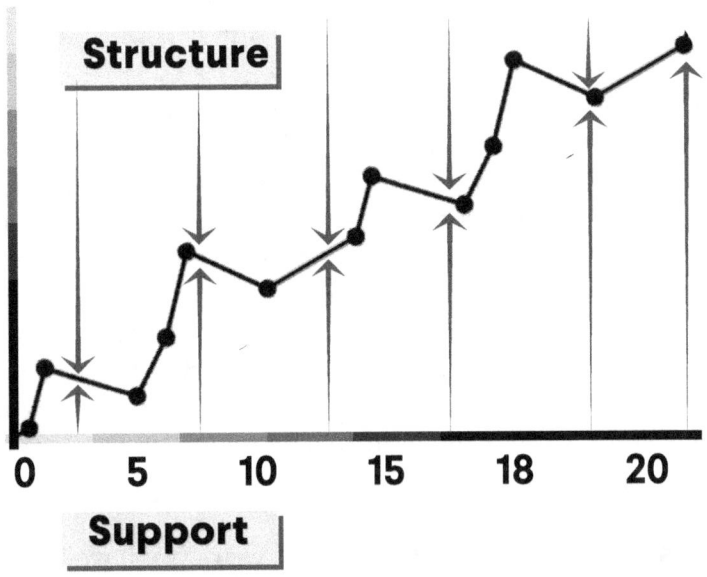

Adult Children in the Home

There are no biblical mandates regarding adult children living with their parents. Each circumstance and context stand on its merit, as the parent and child determine the most practical benefit and God-glorifying solution, knowing the season is transitional. If you have an adult child living in the home, here are three suggestive tips for your consideration.

OBSERVE HIS PRACTICE: What you see in your child is what your child has become. Whether good or bad, what he is today is what he will be should he marry. His practice is his pattern. You must have an accurate understanding of who he is. All parents should practice objective discernment of their children, regardless of the child's age. People do not change at the marriage altar. They continue to be who they have been. Whether the child is 2, 12, or 22, it is important to discern your child so you can help him become more like Jesus. His future bride will thank you if you have the insight to perceive how he is and the courage to speak into his life. As long as he is in your home, your goal is to help him become like Jesus.

ASSESS HIS MATURITY: If the Lord gives you a few more years to help your child mature, it is a bonus. It would be marvelous if all children married after they were mature enough to marry, but that is not always the case. A solid working definition for biblical maturity is to be like Jesus. For two sound and practical templates for what Jesus was like, check out Galatians 5:22-23 and 1 Corinthians 13:4-7. If your child is increasingly approximating the character traits in these two passages, you should feel great about releasing him into the culture as a man who can live well under God's authority.

MEASURE HIS AUTONOMY: Whatever years you have left with him should be spent guiding him out of the nest. You do this by observing his practices while motivating him to a maturity that looks like Jesus—per the two templates in Galatians and 1 Corinthians. When he can be Christlike while living autonomously in God's world, you've completed your job. This child will not need your ongoing surveillance or intervention because he knows how to walk humbly with Jesus. I'm assuming he will permit you to speak into his life while realizing that many children are not humble or self-aware enough to ask for spiritual guidance.

Three Adult Child Tips

Practice, maturity, and autonomy provide a framework for thinking about your ongoing shepherding of your adult child's heart. As you implement these concepts, your goal is for him to leave the nest. Unless there are prohibiting circumstances, you want to release him into God's world. These final three tips will serve you well as you equip your child for the rest of his life.

RESPONSIBILITY: By this time, he should have gainful employment, which is an excellent opportunity for him to practice living on his own and under the authority of others, though he is interdependent. One of the benefits of being in the home is that the parents can be ad hoc life coaches. I would have loved to have had parents who could release me into the world while continuing to tether me to their wisdom and care. I was a survivalist: tossed in the pond of life at an early age and required to sink or swim. If you are an adult child and if your situation is similar to mine, I recommend you find your Paul. Every Timothy needs one. One of the ways you can help your child learn how to live well in God's world is for him to have ever-increasing responsibilities. Think through how to grow his to-do list. Think about what he should be doing as a 45-year-old man with a wife and children, and plot a plan to help him get there.

RULES: We cannot live without rules, and neither can he. There are rules for driving, buying, working, and relaxing. Structure and standards are good concepts that teach us how to function well. Without the reinforcing structure of rules, there would be chaos. If your adult child lives with you, one of the most loving things you can do is clarify the rules in your home. It is your home, not his. Just like it is God's world, not his, he needs to learn how to live as a man under authority—yours and God's. If he humbly obeys and follows your leadership, life will be good for him. If he does not, it is your job to impose the appropriate consequences for his misbehavior.

GUARD: One of your strongest temptations will be to become his mini-messiah. You cannot change your child. Over-worrying about his lack of change or trying to manipulate his life will not work in the way you hope. Typically, there are two ways a parent becomes a mini-messiah. First, the parent will not correct or discipline the child because they want to protect him from pain. The parent does not understand how their lack of obedience by withholding discipline perpetuates the child's lack of obedience. Secondly, the parent will not release the child into the culture. They overprotect him, trying to guard him from dumb mistakes and harsh consequences. Sometimes, it is the Lord's discipline working through the silly errors that bring us to our senses (Luke 15:17).

Call to Action

Marriage and parenting are the two hardest things a person will ever do. To do them well, one must do them with the Lord. So, let me leave you with the best parenting advice you will ever receive. I read this in Paul Miller's book *A Praying Life*: "Pray often for your child." Our best hope is in the transforming gospel. Only the regenerated soul is truly safe in this world and the one to come. Pray to that end.

1. How many children do you have, and how are they different from each other? Understanding their differences is essential in training them in the way that they should go.
2. How would you characterize yourself? Are you too much of a disciplinarian, too permissive, or well-balanced in your parenting? Does your spouse or someone who knows you well agree with you?
3. Do you tend to over-worry about your children? If so, how does it affect you and them? What is your plan to change?
4. Do you have an adult child not walking with the Lord? If so, how much do you struggle with regret about the past or how much future fear do you carry in your soul? If either of these is true, what does that tell you about your theology, and what is your plan to change?

2

Introducing Kids to the World

Every home is a laboratory where parents have the privilege of incrementally introducing their children to the culture around them. This incremental child development process prepares children to live in and engage in their world as adults while not being overcome by the world. The proactive and intentional parent does not wait until the child is an adult to teach them how to live like an adult.

Parental Fear

Parental fear is the most common struggle that caring parents have to deal with daily when it comes to their children. It makes sense to me because I'm one of those parents. I want our children to have a great life. I also want them to love God with all their hearts, souls, and minds (Matthew 22:37-39). I'm aware of my faith-fear tension daily. Some days, I worry, and other days, not so much. Typically, it's their behavior that manipulates my worry, don't worry tension. If they are behaving well, I don't worry. But if they are not acting well, it would not be a stretch to say that I can project their current failures into the rest of their lives.

To think about how our children can control me so

quickly does not speak well about my orthodoxy—faith in God—or my orthopraxy: how I live out my faith in God. However, my weakness does lead me to ponder my parental focus, usually with two incisive diagnostic questions:

- Am I more aware of God's goodness and faithfulness to me when my child is behaving poorly?
- Am I more controlled by my unmet expectations for our child?

How I answer these questions not only determines my levels of worry and anxiousness over our children but also influences how I respond to them. This issue is especially acute when they are not meeting my expectations. What about you? How would you answer those two questions?

Parent Traps

If trusting God is your characterization during parental situational challenges, even though you may not have perfected your trust in God, you will parent with faith, grace, courage, and joy. If your unmet parental expectations regarding your child manage your heart, you will be tempted to succumb to a plethora of parenting traps. Here are six of the more common ones, which I do have some experience with regarding our children.

- Succumb to the temptation to control your child.
- Succumb to the temptation to be dictatorial without appeal.
- Succumb to the temptation to be self-reliant.
- Succumb to the temptation of fear.
- Succumb to the temptation to overreact.
- Succumb to the temptation to over-shelter.

One of the overarching expectations that hover over our

parenting desires is to have the perfect 6-year-old, 10-year-old, or 15-year-old. Without keeping the end in mind, you could become a thorn in your child's flesh as you micro-manage the contours of their fluctuating behaviors throughout the years. Some people call this helicopter parenting, which is an unfortunate term because it lacks biblical clarity—a lack that makes it sound better than what it is. Through a biblical lens, helicopter parenting is more about selfishness, faithlessness, self-reliance, or fear-based parenting. It also shuns the unthinkable possibility that God could be engaging a child in spiritually beneficial ways that appear to fly in the face of your best life now theology.

Faith Through Failure

If anyone comes to me and does not hate his father and mother and wife and children and brothers and sisters, yes, and even his own life, he cannot be my disciple. Whoever does not bear his cross and come after me cannot be my disciple.

(Luke 14:26-27)

If your child becomes an adult who loves God more than he loves himself, his wife, children, or anyone else, you can rest assured that he will be okay regardless of what happens to him. A micro-managing parent will never understand this because their thinking is myopic (2 Peter 1:9). They center their focus on the moment: what is going on with the child right now. There could be several reasons for that kind of fear-motivated parenting.

The parent is fearful of what the child may become, so he implements authoritarian, smothering control. The parent is lazy and disdains inconveniences, so he legislates behavior. The parent is concerned about his reputation, so he demands unquestioned obedience. A gospelized parent is less tense, less stressed, and less angry while more restful in God's sovereign control of all matters, big and small. Rather than trying to iron out all present-day wrinkles in the child's life, he uses those wrinkles to equip the child for the future.

This kind of worldview reminds me of a long list of parents who have come to me seeking help for their children who were bouncing off the walls. Today, many of those children are God-loving adults. During the season of parental uncertainty, the parents were in a tizzy. I typically tell a parent like this how God saved me when I was 25 years old. Ten years earlier, I was in jail. What you are seeing in your child should not derail your faith in what God can do. I'm not saying God will save your child because He does not regenerate every person. Some children do reject God, live a life of rebellion, die, and go to eternal Hell. Then, other children experience conversion as adults, like me.

Religious Motives

Though it's more pleasant not to consider these truths, we must not bury our collective heads in the sand and play pretend. We live in a fallen world. Some people choose to stay in their fallenness, a truth that does not diminish the goodness of God, though it should motivate all parents to reassess their reasons for loving God.

- Do you love God when your children do not love God?
- Do you mature in faith when your children are living in disobedience?
- Do you carry ongoing guilt for your parental mistakes?
- What needs to happen in your heart to be free from the guilt of parental mistakes?
- Does your faith rise or fall according to your parenting successes and failures, or do the works of Jesus stabilize your soul?

Trying to manage the future outcomes of your children will always backfire. If the temptation to control, smother, dictate, or overly legislate your children's lives, I appeal to you to reconsider. If you are isolating them from the culture —where they will spend their adult lives—I call on you to rethink your parenting methodology. The little people in your home will only be in your home for a nano-second. They may spend ninety percent of their lives outside of your parental jurisdiction. Equipping them for the future is one of the most useful things you could do as a parent to help them live well in the world, which will make up nearly all of their earthly existence.

Sheltering Children

My friend Willy came from Cameroon when he was 19 years old. It was overwhelming in many ways. Willy had no preparation for what our Americanized world was offering him. It was a struggle for him to adjust to a country where he was not equipped to live. He was a foreigner. The best-case scenario for Willy would have been a season of American culture indoctrination while he was still living in his home country, Cameroon. The good news was that God led him to a good local church that befriended, served, helped, and equipped him to live well as a Christian in our American culture.

Everyone is not as fortunate as Willy. Some parents rear their children in fear-based contexts that perpetuate dysfunction. They identify the taboos in the culture around them and isolate their children from them without realizing the importance of incrementally and biblically introducing them to the culture they inhabit. These children grow up socially awkward, culturally disengaged, and evangelistically hindered because of their sheltered childhood. They live with inordinate fears about the culture, borne out of ignorance, poor parenting, and bad theology.

Jesus had scores of unsaved friends. Wait a minute! All of His friends were unsaved. Jesus came to an unsaved world to live in it, engage it, and serve it, to convert it (Philippians 2:5-11). His missionary efforts in our culture are a legend. There have been books written about how He lived in the world while not overcome by the world. The socially awkward, ill-prepared child cannot be like Jesus. He will have to create a holy huddle that is sequestered from the culture while dropping Bible tracts like bread crumbs that hopefully will lead those outside his camp to their church doors. What he can't do is penetrate his culture with the gospel of Christ. He's afraid to, and his parents never equipped him to live in the world.

Worldly Introductions

When I say introducing your child to the world, I am not talking about teaching them to curse, drink beer, watch porn, smoke cigarettes, and do other sin-festive things like what our culture does. I am talking about familiarizing your child with the ways of the world while teaching him how not to imbibe it. Some of the future adult goals for children are not to be surprised, repulsed, or tempted by the culture that they will step into as young adults. If you don't teach them how to do this, like a child reaching up to touch the hot stove because he did not know it was hot, the culture will burn his hand. The thing you meticulously kept from him will hurt him.

Your home is a laboratory. You should continually stretch and challenge your children so you can understand them better while teaching them more effectively. If you have more than one child, you know very well about their uniqueness, which is why you cannot do cookie-cutter parenting. For example, to say that alcohol is evil and you'll go to Hell if you drink it is fear-motivated parental ignorance. While you may bind the conscience of one child, as he treats alcohol like a plague, your next child may not be so motivated. Children need loving instruction, not fear-laced tactics.

Each child needs your time, nurturing, instruction, and biblical clarity. You do this by talking to them, asking them diverse questions while motivating them according to how God has made them (Proverbs 22:6). You discern where each child is spiritually, mentally, and emotionally. You seek to determine their theological awareness and their intuition to pick up on scriptural truths. With these kinds of assessments, you begin plotting a trajectory that will lead them to the cross and into the culture. Christ came to where we were. He converted us to His way of thinking and told us to go into all the world (Matthew 28:19-20; Luke 24:49).

Children Under Bushels

You want to do similarly: engage, envision, and equip them to enter the mission field.

- Do you have a good working knowledge of how God created your child?
- Do you give blanket edicts to your children, not considering their uniqueness?
- How are you customizing your parenting to each child?

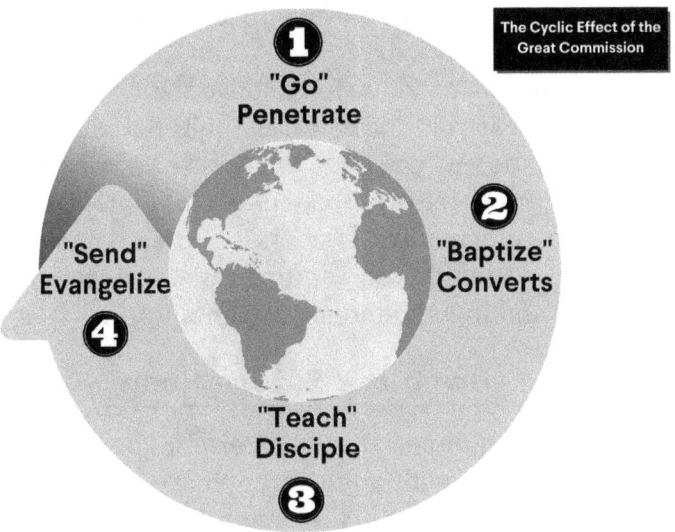

If you are not already, I appeal to you to think from an eschatological perspective. Stretch your children. Give them opportunities to succeed and fail. Your home is a laboratory where it's not about passing or failing. It's a training ground where both passing and failing are opportunities to emulate Christ. If your child succeeds, you want to discern any self-righteous or self-reliant tendencies. Success is an excellent opportunity to identify, isolate, and affirm humility. It's the test of prosperity. If your child fails, you can encourage him by showing him what went wrong and why it went wrong. You can teach him how to discern the heart issues that typically accompany failure, i.e., fear, self-reliance, or perfectionism.

Failure and success are pictures of their future lives. They will win; they will lose. You have a fantastic opportunity to walk them through these outcomes today while equipping them to live well in the future. Sheltering is an essential part of parenting. Parents understand this, but sheltering and fear-based protection should never be the totality of a child's life. If it is, your children will be culturally confused and spiritually tempted when their time comes to stand without your guidance.

It may seem prudent and convenient to shelter your children. But if you do, beware: You'll be hard-pressed to know them the way you need to because you never set them up for success or failure. You will learn about your children when the testing comes. It's better to create those contexts while they are with you rather than waiting for them to leave you, and they flounder in their culture.

Bring the Future Home

One way we equipped our children for the future was by connecting them with adults. They have always socialized with adults ever since they could walk and talk. We understood that we had less than two decades to instruct them and that they would likely have 70+ years in an adult world, so we strategically and appropriately gave them a few adults to interact with while they were young. Like all children, they naturally gravitated to their kind: other kids. Thus, we had to be intentional by connecting them with older, bigger, and wiser people. Small groups in the local church were good and safe places for this kind of adult training. Hospitality was also an excellent context.

I hope that you ask the Spirit to illuminate your thinking with some practical ways you can prepare your child to live well in their future lives. Parenting is hard work. Duh! This challenge is why your first call to action is to ask God how to proceed. Each situation, family, and child are different. Though I do not believe what we did is best for you, here are a few things we did with our children. They are merely suggestive. You must ask the Spirit and a few competent leaders for advice; they know you and your children and should have wise input for things you can do to introduce them to the world.

- Theology: We began teaching our children Systematic Theology (ST) when they were four and five years old. We taught them specific theological concepts, such as omnipotence, omniscience, omnipresence, anthropomorphic expressions, and hypostatic union.
- Finances: We set up bank accounts for each of them when they were about five years old. They loved getting the suckers from the bank tellers, too.
- Culture: At a young age, we watched dramas and documentaries that showed real life. They learned about drugs, alcohol, and other cultural problems while teaching them the importance of the law and respect for all people, including police officers.
- Language: When we had the sex talk, I started teaching them a theology of language, including cursing, which also addressed motivations of the heart.

Call to Action

1. There are many ways to introduce your children to the world long before they enter the world. Why is this a wise approach to parenting?
2. What are some of the pitfalls of not envisioning them about the contexts where they will spend most of their lives?
3. What are at least five more ways you could introduce your child to the world?

3

Teach Your Children to Curse

It is impossible to engage our culture at any level and not hear their language, including curse words. Whether it is social media, a television show, or a stroll in the park, our culture's words do not discriminate or care about our sensibilities or worldview. Because of the unending assault of their language upon us, the questions every caring parent must answer are: Who is going to teach their child the culture's language, and when is the proper time to do it?

A Time to Lead

A few relevant and practical questions about parenting, children, and language will help us orient our minds and establish our goals regarding this critical subject.

- Will your child learn curse words from someone? If so, who will teach your child curse words?
- From what context do you want your child to learn their first curse words?
- Who will be developing your child's theology of language, including curse words?
- Who is currently teaching your child a theology of curse words?

Our culture's words are like soldiers on a mission to redefine and reshape how we think. Their language has a clear-cut objective: to defile and corrupt the soul. This concept was made too real to me some years ago when our then-six-year-old daughter verbalized her joy at some good fortune that came her way. She was talking to our 45-year-old friend, who was not prepared for the moment, when our child exclaimed, "I am so damn excited." She made that statement while flinging her arms upward and falling backward inside our van. My friend's mouth dropped as she helplessly tried to regain her game face. Our innocent daughter was oblivious to the weight of her words. That was the day I made a mental note to teach her about curse words.

It became clear she needed a better theology and practice of language. Somehow she picked up on the word damn and unwittingly used it in context. All wise and discerning parents are well aware that our culture will not slow down for them to catch up and that it is more than willing to do our job for us. Someone will teach your child about what is right and wrong. Will it be you or them? When the world inevitably knocks on your door, it would be proactively wise of you to have already introduced your children to it. With language in mind, here are four things children need to think well about our culture's language.

- They need a biblical interpretation of the culture's words.
- They need a lack of surprise or curiosity by the culture's words.
- They need the courage to not imitate and walk away from the culture's language.
- They need discretion when using the culture's language in relational interactions.

Threefold Goal

Let no corrupting talk come out of your mouths, but only such as is good for building up, as fits the occasion, that it may give grace to those who hear. (Ephesians 4:29).

This kind of training begins with a transcending and overarching parenting goal, which is to love God and others as we love ourselves (Matthew 22:36-40). As your child is learning this unique two-tiered worldview about loving God and others, you can begin laying down a sound language strategy. That strategy will have three parts: Teach, Test, and Release.

- Teach your child what God's Word says (or implies) about language.
- Test how your child is using language in relational contexts.
- Release your child incrementally into the world for the practical application of your teaching.

With your God-loving, other-centered worldview in place, you will be able to instruct your child to rise above the unedifying noise of our culture. To turn language training over to someone who does not believe the way you do would be disobedient and unkind. Thus, I waited until our "cursing daughter" was 11 years old before we began our theology of curse word conversations. Our son was 12 years old when I started introducing him to swear words. Our youngest daughter was going on 12, too. These private conversations were between the child and their parents, while the younger siblings were not part of those discussions.

A Time to Cuss

Our children had proven themselves trustworthy in stewarding truths about less weighty matters, so introducing them to weightier things like our culture's language was not a concern for us. We were confident they would be able to steward our conversations with discretion and humility. This season is a wisdom issue that each parent will have to determine according to the season of life and maturity of the child. As our kids were advancing to a higher level in school (and church), there was motivation for us to be proactive in cultural language indoctrination lessons, knowing they would be encountering new words with more culturally indoctrinated children.

I initially introduced five words to our daughter and defined them. They were curse, cuss, hell, damn, and ass. Typically, when we have conversations like this, I use a writing device so I can sketch them for them to see visually. I wrote the words "cuss words" on our tablet and asked her if she knew what they meant. She did not. I then wrote the words curse words, and she did not know what they meant either. From there, I introduced her to the words hell, damn, and ass. She asked, "Why does dam have an 'n' at the end of it?" A part of me was sad because I knew I was moving her from childhood innocence to being an adult in our culture.

Many parents struggle with the idea of their children getting older and leaving the nest. I did. It is hard to accept and even tougher to release them into the wild (world). However, I have come to terms with the inevitability of life while choosing to be the one guiding them out of the nest rather than the world luring them from of the nest (Deuteronomy 32:11). We continued as we talked about Hell being a place of eternal torment and how some individuals could use it as an unkind and angry response, as in, "Go to hell!" It was interesting she did not know what a burro was and had never heard the word ass in the context of a donkey.

Theology of Language

I did tell her how butt and crack were words that referred to ass and how buttock is the correct term for a rear-end. She was already familiar with the words penis and vagina, names we chose to use with them when they were toddlers. It seemed appropriate to end our first language training session with those five words, though I did let her know we would revisit this conversation in the future as we look at more of the culture's words. The main thing I wanted her to learn was not the words as much as the wisdom, respect, discretion, humility, and courage needed to think biblically about our culture's language.

We spent a lot of time talking about the theology of language and how words begin with a neutral and innocuous fact. Words are made alive and given force by the presupposition, motive, and meaning we give to them. Our presupposition is the lens through which we bring meaning to a word. Motive determines how we use a word. We derive the meaning from the interpretation attached to the word. The word Trinity is neutral to a two-year-old who has never heard the word. But after you teach the child how the Trinity is a way of thinking about God, the word is animated. To the God-lover, it is incredibly, wonderfully, amazingly, and overwhelmingly stupendous.

You could use the word switch as an analogy for words. A switch is just a switch, nothing more and nothing less, except when my father told me to go outside and get a switch from a tree so he could swat me with it. A switch was no longer neutral to me. The past abuse of a switch in my life affects how I think about a switch today. You may understand a switch differently, as a utilitarian device to turn lights on and off. Though electrical switches were part of my childhood, too, there was a darker, more dangerous application of the word switch. Typically, the first person to define the word will have more influence over how a child thinks about the word.

Take Crap, for Example

Thomas Crapper became a famous plumber in London circa 1900. He did not invent the flush toilet, but he did invent the ballcock, and his name was on many of the manhole covers throughout London. He was known for being a plumber. His name has since become synonymous with a bowel movement. I suspect most of you have heard the phrase, "I'm going to take a crap." Suppose I was a famous plumber circa 1900, and my name became synonymous with toilet paraphernalia. Today, people would say, "I'm going to take a thom," and some people would think that kind of talk is crude, uncouth, and unsophisticated.

But they might use the words crapper and crap, or maybe they would give a child the word Crappy as a nickname, and it would not sound wrong to anyone. Someone may say, "I'm going to knock the 'thom' out of you," and it would sound harsh, and perhaps a fight would ensue. A few of our good Christian folk would be offended by such language as Thomas or Thom. Language evolves, and what once was is no more. How we interpret words (meaning) and use words (motive) affects how we think about and react to them. Some of the old Puritan writers talked about intercourse with God. We do not talk that way today for obvious reasons.

The King James Bible tells about bastard children (Hebrews 12:8) and pissing on a wall (1 Samuel 25:22), but those words have evolved to the point where it is considered archaic, crass, and crude to use them. Understanding the motives and intentions behind words should free our consciences to teach our children a theology of bad words. Suppose your motivations were right, and your intentions were pure. If so, then you are the perfect person to teach your children bad words. You are not trying to hurt or twist your child but to free your child from cultural terminology and temptations.

- Is your conscience free to lead your child through bad language?
- Are you mature enough to teach your child curse words?

What Are You Exporting?

Paul talked about giving grace to those who hear, which is a vital truth when thinking about words. Does your language give grace? Do your words build up? Are your words redemptive? What are you trying to export to your children? Our children learned not only the words of our culture and what they mean but also how and when to use the world's language. It takes more maturity to use words correctly and biblically than to use them harmfully. You can walk through any crowded public venue and realize that people do not know how to use words redemptively. They know words, but they do not know how to use them to build up others.

This abuse of words should motivate any parent to take the lead in language learning. If you do not teach them the culture's words and their meanings, plus the motives behind them, the surrogate cultural parents, i.e., social media, who have no shame or discretion, will do your job. Your children will not always watch G and PG movies or live in a G and PG world. The Christian parent hopes that when the world comes knocking, their children will not be vulnerable to its temptations or terminology but will be able to intelligently, humbly, courageously, and wisely engage in the culture while not succumbing to it.

Worldly Addendum

Do not love the world or the things in the world. If anyone loves the world, the love of the Father is not in him. For all that is in the world—the desires of the flesh and the desires of the eyes and pride in possessions—is not from the Father but is from the world.

(1 John 2:15-16)

You cannot talk about words without talking about worldliness. Worldliness—biblically defined—is not so much in the world as it is in our hearts. John was clear in his first epistle about how worldliness is inside of us, not outside of us. (See also James 1:14-15.) John identifies worldliness as desires and pride, not some object or thing in our culture. Words are not worldly things in our culture unless our evil hearts take them and make them wrong by uploading evil motives for evil purposes. As cultures and epochs change, so do our words. The careful Christian is in tune with the culture in which they live and uses words that are fitting to being a Christian in that culture.

Call to Action

1. *Do not be hung up about words.* Words are words. You do not have to giggle when you say penis, and you do not have to feel as though you have gotten away with something when you say damn.

2. *Consider your audience.* Do your words uplift and build up, or do they degrade and tear down? The gospel is more about others than about us. Always think of others. Never use your freedom as a right to do as you please.

3. *What is your motive?* When you speak, make sure the gospel saturates your heart. Let the words of your mouth come from a heart treasure that has been marinating in the gospel. If so, your speech will be redemptive.

4. *Are you a crude dude?* Regularly give yourself sober assessments. What feedback have those closest to you given you? How do they perceive, understand, and think about your speech patterns?

5. *Have your words weighed.* Most people will not give honest and critical feedback about the deeper matters of the heart. You will have to pursue it. Do not be afraid to seek out your friends to serve you with their assessment of your speech patterns.

6. *Are you an encourager?* Do the people around you feel more encouraged or discouraged after spending time with you? How does your speech affect others? Are you characterized as a redemptive builder by your words?

4

Teach Your Son to Be a Husband

Statistically speaking, the chances of your son or daughter being married are greater than them spending their adult lives as singles. This likelihood is not inside information but public knowledge. Boys like girls and girls like boys, and most boys and girls will tie the knot in holy matrimony, even though there has been a multi-decade assault on marriage between a man and woman. How do you prepare your son to be an excellent future husband to a wonderful lady? When would you begin? My answers may surprise you.

Passive and Active

Though the idea of marriage is becoming more and more confusing in our culture, it's still a popular notion, especially in the Christian community. Every parent has approximately two decades to prepare a son (or daughter) for the most challenging, rewarding, and extended relational adventure that they will experience. We call it marriage. You may not know what your child will do vocationally; you may not know where he will live, but you should assume he will marry someone.

Think of the early years of a child's life as training years.

It's how you would consider anything that you value. For example, if you want to become an engineer after college, you don't wait until you're old enough to apply for an engineering job downtown. You begin plotting a course that will lead you to the eventual day when you can get the job of your dreams. Marriage is no different. However, the problem with marriage is that a child does not have the capacity or common sense to chart such a course. This problem is why there are parents. A child's dad and mom are life coaches who have the responsibility and opportunity to give a child experienced marital training to get him ready for that special day when they tie the knot. Parents wear many hats, and perhaps none is more significant than that of a trainer.

To Teach or Not

To teach or not to teach is not the question. You are the parent, and your child will learn how to think and behave based on the equipping that you give him, which starts with how you live your life. You are a living, breathing example that is teaching him something each day of his life. I recall asking a teenager if he wanted to get married in a few years. He said, "No." I asked him why, and he responded by saying that the dysfunction in his family was so frustrating that he would never marry. Though his parents did not train him biblically, they did train him. Their poor example unwittingly motivated him to reject the idea of marriage altogether. He may change his mind in the future—after he meets that amazing lady—but at the time we were talking, he did not want anything to do with marriage. His parents trained an anti-marriage worldview into him because of their marital hostility and familial dysfunction.

Regrettably, if he does marry, he will not have the training he needs to do it well. Nearly all the marriage counseling I have done involved the parents' adverse shaping effects on their children. The parents were not the cause of any of these children's future marital problems, but they were a significant shaping influence—even if the adverse impact was from one parent. It only takes one ineffective parent to impact a child's future marriage negatively.

Active Training Years

Parents rub off on their children. They are training them—at least passively. One of the best gifts you can give your child is to take the bull by the horns by actively exporting a Christlike example and Jesus-centered instruction to him. For example, I do not recommend waiting for the marriage ceremony to explain the art of husbandry to your son. If he has not learned how to be a husband by the time he becomes one, he will have to go into rapid OJT mode (on-the-job training). Your first ten years with your son (dependent to interdependent years) are the best opportunities to teach him the art of husbandry. As he moves toward the end of his interdependent years (ten to twenty) and into independent living, your job will be to affirm and adjust any good or bad habits he has learned from the first decade of his life.

1. A child's dependent phase is from zero to two.
2. A child's interdependent phase is from two to twenty-two.
3. A child's independent phase is the rest of his life.

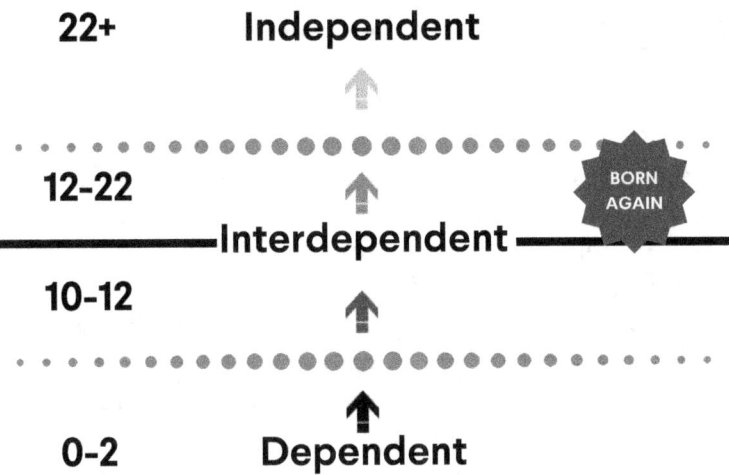

The early years will be your son's most attentive and pliable years. As he moves into the teen phase of his life, he will want to distance himself from you by exploring and experimenting with who he is. He needs to discover himself with minimal parental control. He is itching to do this, and if you don't give him space and freedom to be who he is, you'll complicate these years. Your influence will slowly lose its effectiveness. If you have been positive, intentional, and actively training, he may still want your advice. If you have been a negative and passive trainer, he will resist your efforts to instruct him after he launches into an incremental, independent lifestyle.

Learning

Likewise, husbands, live with your wives in an understanding way, showing honor to the woman as the weaker vessel, since they are heirs with you of the grace of life, so that your prayers may not be hindered.

(1 Peter 3:7)

There are many things you can teach a son about the art of husbandry. Three of those—in sequential order—are learning, loving, and leading. All three flow out of 1 Peter 3:7, the "how to be a good husband" verse. Fortunately, our son had three women in our home to ply his future trade. Since he was about three years old, I told him how he treats the women in our family would be a snapshot of how he would treat his future wife. We knew that our son would not be profoundly different in attitude, words, and actions with his future wife than he was with his sisters and mother—after the honeymoon wears off, of course. If he were selfish now, he would be selfish then. If he were a servant now, he would be a servant then. I wanted him to learn how to make practical applications of the gospel with his sisters and mother while in the training lab—our home.

If he could master the practicalized gospel in these relationships, he would be in an excellent position to do marriage well. One of those practical data points was serving. Jesus did not come to earth for others to serve Him (Mark 10:45). If our son could learn this singular aspect of the gospel, he would be a rock star in his future marriage. Paul said it another way when he appealed to us to count others more significant than ourselves (Philippians 2:3). A few questions under the category of learning will help you assess how well you are guiding your son.

- How has the gospel affected your son?
- Is he a gospel-centered learner?
- How is his affection for the gospel affecting his family?
- Does he seek to understand his parents and siblings to serve them?

Loving

Love is patient and kind; love does not envy or boast; it is not arrogant or rude. It does not insist on its way; it is not irritable or resentful; it does not rejoice at wrongdoing but rejoices with the truth. Love bears all things, believes all things, hopes all things, endures all things.

(1 Corinthians 13:4-7)

The call on his life was to not only understand the females in our home by learning them, but he must know what it means to put what he has learned into practice: he must love them. Paul gave us a template for what love looks like in 1 Corinthians 13:4-7. As you read this passage, note the fifteen pieces of evidence for biblical love and think through how to teach them to your son. How would you answer the questions regarding your son from the love chapter?

- Is your son patient?
- Is your son kind?
- Does your son envy?
- Does your son boast?
- Is your son arrogant?
- Is your son rude?
- Does your son insist on his way?
- Is your son irritable?
- Is your son resentful?
- Does your son rejoice in wrongdoing?
- Does your son rejoice in the truth?
- Does your son bear all things?
- Does your son believe all things (thinks the best of others)?
- Does your son hope all things?
- Does your son endure all things?

Who wants to marry a millionaire? If these concepts are how your son loves others—especially his wife—he will be a rich man, and she will be overwhelmingly blessed. Your goal is to train these things into your son to the point where his thoughts, attitudes, words, and actions have a love reflex to them. What you're looking for initially is the presence of these traits rather than the perfection of them.

FIVE-POINT LEADERSHIP ANALYSIS

MASTERMIND TRAINING PROGRAM

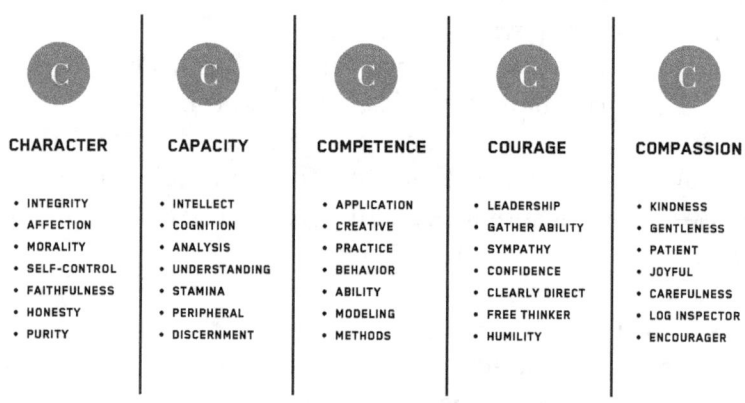

CHARACTER	CAPACITY	COMPETENCE	COURAGE	COMPASSION
• INTEGRITY	• INTELLECT	• APPLICATION	• LEADERSHIP	• KINDNESS
• AFFECTION	• COGNITION	• CREATIVE	• GATHER ABILITY	• GENTLENESS
• MORALITY	• ANALYSIS	• PRACTICE	• SYMPATHY	• PATIENT
• SELF-CONTROL	• UNDERSTANDING	• BEHAVIOR	• CONFIDENCE	• JOYFUL
• FAITHFULNESS	• STAMINA	• ABILITY	• CLEARLY DIRECT	• CAREFULNESS
• HONESTY	• PERIPHERAL	• MODELING	• FREE THINKER	• LOG INSPECTOR
• PURITY	• DISCERNMENT	• METHODS	• HUMILITY	• ENCOURAGER

Perhaps the this graphic will assist with thinking about character traits and attitudes. If you plant the seeds of these ideas in his little heart, you will have a decade to mature them into a harvest of love. The best approach is to teach him one concept at a time so that you don't overwhelm him or over-expect too much from him. As you teach him, you will have many opportunities to observe and encourage him. Each time he nails it, you want to draw attention to what he did. Motivate him with grace by identifying and isolating the evidence of God's good work in his life. Affirming words build up and motivate while assuring him that he is doing it right.

- Does your son spontaneously serve others?
- Describe how you see his heart of love for others.
- Does he have manners in that he knows how to honor and show respect?

Leading

A great leader will take the time to study (learn) his audience and then seek to serve (love) them based on what he has learned about them. A self-centered person will only think about himself, and his desire to do things will be about his selfish pleasures. You will find everything I've said about loving in the leadership style of Jesus. He became like us (Philippians 2:7) so that He could understand us (Hebrews 4:15) to love us (Hebrews 2:14-15). There is no more extraordinary model for leadership than Jesus, and if your son learns to emulate the life of Christ, he will be a fantastic leader husband. You can begin your early assessment of him by asking these three diagnostic questions:

1. **LEADER:** What kind of leader is your son today?
2. **LEARNING:** Is he more interested in himself or others? Does he mostly study himself or others?
3. **LOVING:** Is his love mostly self-centered or others-centered?

You should never ask whether your son is a leader. He is. Every person—male or female—is a leader. The question to ask is about the kind of leader he is. What kind of leader is he choosing to be right now? This worldview is why you want to teach him how to practice an others-centered lifestyle. If he chooses a self-centered leadership style, he will perpetuate frustration in his relationships while sucking the life out of his future marriage. Any saved, sane, humble, and wise woman would love to follow a man who spends his days counting others more significant than himself and who knows how to care for her practically.

Let's Get Practical

I gave you a practical template to teach your son in 1 Corinthians 13:4-7. It provides snapshots of the life of Christ, which is why it is so powerful. A good practice is to write down those points and do a personal assessment of your son. Identify his strengths and weaknesses. Discern the kind of person he is today, which will give you the starting point to develop him into a competent future husband. With your starting point nailed down and Christ in view, you can begin plotting your course that will equip him for the rest of his life. If you are not currently modeling the life you want him to live, you have a new starting point. It would be hypocritical and disastrous to attempt to teach your son something you are not trying to perfect in your life. If you attempt to bypass the personal modeling of Christ, he will more than likely reject you and the Christ you hope he will emulate.

As you do these things, remember that your most powerful parenting tool is prayer. Do your best to train your son, but never forget that if your child transforms, it will be because of God's grace. Awful parents can have God-loving children, and good parents can have Christ-rejecting children. Realizing you're operating under God's sovereignty and mysterious grace is not a call for sloppy parenting practices. It should keep you from over-trying and over-worrying about the results. Leave the results to God. Your job is to water and plant a discipleship worldview into your child.

Call to Action

1. Before addressing your child's strengths and weaknesses, what are yours? Are there areas that you need to address? If so, what are they, and how do you plan to change them—if you need to change? If you do need to change something, please ask a friend to assist you.

2. Work through the 1 Corinthian 13 template, assessing yourself. Perhaps you're unsure of an area where you need to change. Applying those concepts to your attitude, words, and actions may spur you in the right direction.

3. Some parents need to repent to their children before initiating something like what I'm asking you to do with your child. You want to be humble if your parenting has not emulated the 1 Corinthians 13:4-7 standard. If you share your failures with and seek forgiveness from your child, it could open a world of opportunity for you to be the leader that he needs.

5

My Son Has Three Practice Wives

The wedding day is not the best time to learn how to be a spouse. Too many young couples begin this way. Without prior marriage training, they had to figure out how to get along with each other in the school of hard knocks. Some of them do not endure their marriage, which is why we chose to give our son three wives. If practice makes perfect, the assumption is that we could help him get close to what it means to be a biblical husband—should that day come.

Husband Practice

No, we have not joined the Mormon faith, and we're not polygamists. I have one wife, and she's sufficient—praise God. One's enough. Two is too many. Three's a crowd, but our son is different. He's in training. He has been in marriage training since he was about three years old. The hope is that by the time he ties the knot, the art of husbandry will be like painting by numbers. Three practice wives will give him many opportunities to get his reps in. We figured if he could get along with the three ladies in our home—his mom and two sisters—he would have the necessary up-fitting to marry a young lady to love, learn, and lead her well.

I introduced this notion of three wives to him as wearing leg weights (Hebrews 12:1-2). After you remove them, you feel like you can run forever. During his childhood, he persevered under the burden of his three practice wives. An explanation may be helpful. Every home is a tight, inescapable community where sinners live elbow to elbow with each other. How each family member treats the other members is a snapshot of their strengths, weaknesses, qualities, and quirks. The paying attention parent sees these relational clues in their children, which signal areas where work must happen to make each other a better, relational human being.

Marriage Reveals

A marriage certificate will not make a person mature or immature. The wedding day sets the long-term context for people to be who they were before the wedding. There is no upgrade when a guy becomes a husband. Whatever he brings to the wedding day will determine the kind of marriage he and his wife will have. This perspective applies to girls, too. Some dating and newlywed couples do not understand this perspective. They fall prey to myopic love, which restricts them from seeing beyond what's in the moment. The good news is that they can see into their mate's past—beyond the hot date because each one has a history. There were shaping influences that molded them into the people they are today. Sadly, after the honey drips from the honeymoon, myopia burns off, and reality bites hard.

Ladies, the man you married is like a long train with many baggage cars. Just because you were not aware of his baggage—or chose to ignore it—it does not mean that it never existed. A parent could help their child to avoid this problem if they provide the appropriate training in the art of marriage while the child is young. I'm speaking from an under-the-sun perspective because even proactive practice will ultimately not bring what the child needs. It's by grace that any of us is doing anything well, but you don't want to presume against God's grace by not being all you should be for your child.

Future Prep

Sadly, most parents are concerned more with their child's college choice than equipping them for the most important and longest relationship they will ever have. They steer him to the ideal university and motivate him down a prospective vocational track, but too often, they don't equip him to be a spouse. This miscalculation is why a son should practice the art of husbandry long before becoming one. Here are five of the more common responses when I bring up this concept.

- He'll figure it out after he snags a wife.
- We require him to go to premarital counseling for this.
- I've never thought about teaching the art of husbandry before marriage.
- Ain't no big deal! Nobody ever taught me.
- I don't know how to do that.

Most boys who do not learn to respect, honor, and serve the women in their home will not intuitively pick up on these concepts after marriage. These character traits are habits. Like all habits, they take repetition to become second nature. A boy's home is the perfect laboratory to teach and test, hoping to release him into the best version of himself when he's older. Think about some of your bad habits. You can trace most of the roots back to your childhood. Many of our unappealing traits started as children. Why not use that time to build healthy biblical habits into the psyche (soul) of a child?

A Boy's Kryptonite

The similarity between childhood and marriage is striking. Both are two long-term relational constructs. The child is within a family dynamic where he learns interpersonal and relational skills. One of the most important things he will gain as a child is how to humbly, practically, and wisely respond to sin, which is everyone's kryptonite. His immediate family will give him ample opportunities to sin, and they will respond in kind. Sinning is what fallen people do. Living well with other fallen people is the most challenging thing you'll ever do, which is why some folks choose to isolate themselves from others. Living well with others is the ultimate litmus test of a person's maturity—especially those inescapable situations.

If external relationships turn sour, you can unfriend them and find new ones. A child can't leave his family—at least not as quickly as some of them would like to exit. Some teens talk about how they can't wait to get out of the home. They are marking the days until the great emancipation. They typically choose college, military, girlfriends, or careers. They don't perceive their shortsightedness or factor in how the doctrine of sin is their core problem. Even worse, they don't see how the next long-term relationship will be a different dance but a similar song. They may leave the home, but they take their baggage with them.

The Golfer's Fantasy

These kids live in a golfer's fantasy. The retiree shanks the ball on the number seven hole and says, "I'll get it right on the next one." There is always one more hole to play, even after the eighteenth, because there is still tomorrow. Though the scratch golfer can live in his dream world, it will prove disastrous for the immature relationship expert to stay there. I've heard some of these disillusioned teens say, "I didn't choose my parents or my siblings, but I can choose my wife. When I get to make the decision, things will be different." Sin does not care who's doing the picking. It corrupts all people—completely. (See Romans 3:10-12; 5:12.) You may feel better about being in charge, but you will soon learn that you were a primary contributor to your past dysfunction.

There have been millions of young people who jumped from the frying pan of a disappointing home life into the fire of a disappointing marriage. They thought the primary problem was the other person (Matthew 7:3-5). Then, they married another sinner—the only type you can marry. Guess what? The old patterns resurfaced. The baggage is back. They blamed their parents. Now, they blame their spouse. Some of these ignorant adult children choose to divorce; it's a golfer's fantasy. Of course, sin will be waiting, crouching at the door of the next relationship. Fallenness is the tie that binds all Adamic people together.

Practice for Life

Train up a child in the way he should go; even when he is old he will not depart from it.

(Proverbs 22:6)

Children need a sin plan. The first step in implementing a sound sin plan is in the home. One way you can think about this is to use marriage, husband, and wife language when you talk to your children. Let this language be a steady drumbeat in the home, which applies to a son or daughter. Discuss and demonstrate what it means to relate to a husband or wife within the marriage construct. For example, teach your son to open the car door for his mother. If he has a sister, talk to him about serving her, too. When he's entering a building with the females in the family, train him to stop, grab the door, and open it for the ladies. There are many other ways to do this, like not talking over each other in the home, never hitting another sibling, or looking her in the eye when talking to her rather than your phone.

Of course, no yelling or name-calling are no-brainers. Self-control, restraint, and discretion are golden jewels in all relationships. The most effective means to equip a son with the skill of husbandry is for him to imitate his father. Pictures have a much more powerful impact than words. A dad's teaching is secondary and supplementary to how he treats his wife and girls in the home. If he acts like Jesus to them, it will profoundly shape that little boy. If he does not, the adverse effects are powerfully and potentially devastatingly real and long-lasting.

Focus on the Heart

Imagine a child receiving eighteen to twenty years of marriage messaging about the art of husbandry. Your steady stream of messages about being kind and thoughtful toward the opposite sex could become so ingrained that he'd never depart from what he learned from his home laboratory. The primary things you are looking for in your children are the heart attitudes they exhibit toward each other. It's possible to teach them rote behaviors, which could transform them into a relational legalist if you don't address the heart behind the actions. There is a world of difference between a spouse ticking the box of right relational responses versus one who has a deep affection for the other person.

Some of these heart attitudes are honor, love, and respect. I have already mentioned self-control, restraint, and discretion, which are observable fruits of those heart attitudes. The most accurate way to measure a child's heart attitude is by his reactions when he's not getting his way. There will be times when he's having a bad day, and in other instances, a family member will be mean to him. Both situations are snapshots of his future marriage. By observing his current attitudinal responses, you can make at least two conclusions:

- How he responds now is how he will react in the future when his wife is selfish and irritable.
- How he is responding today gives you the data you need to prepare him for his future marriage.

Do Not Miss This

Outdo one another in showing honor.
(Romans 12:10)

It's vital to wrap up these concepts by circling back to the most crucial relational training you will ever give your child. If you're not modeling the person that you want your son to become, all of this will fall flat in one of two ways. He will reject your relationship teaching if you're not practically practicing what you're telling him to be. Or he will choose to be different from you, which could be a better version, but his reactions will come from a heart of anger and self-righteous comparing, not because he's head over heels in love with God and others. Let him see you honoring your wife, experience your affection for your wife, and, by your example (Mark 10:45), let him know what sacrificial serving looks like. Let him biblically compete with you as you both try to outdo each other in loving the women in your home.

If you have girls, treat them as wives. Let them experience what it is like to be cherished, nourished, loved, respected, honored, served, and led. It provides the right view of what a biblical man should be, providing them images of what to look for when the time comes to marry someone. If daughters experience this from you, they probably won't crave it from boys. You should be their man. Show them what biblical manhood is like by your example to them and their mother. Please don't leave them to speculate on these matters. Be clear by the life you display before them in your home.

Call to Action

Yes, we joked around about our son having three wives, but he also knew it was serious business. We cherished the women in our home. We didn't presume on them. We sought ways to serve them. We wanted them to feel our love and affection. It was part of being a man to lead and protect a woman. When Lucia and I go out on a date, I have told our son many times, "You're the leader. You take care of the girls." He loved stepping up to this responsibility. He loved practicing being the man. Someday, he will be the man in marriage.

1. Describe the relational dynamics in your home.
2. What are the positive things?
3. What are some areas that need improvement?
4. What are your specific plans and steps to implement those required changes?

6

Introducing the Talk to Your Child

Is there a terrific way to introduce the sex talk to your child? Every parent is faced with the challenge, though every parent does not think about sex the same way. Of course, there are a few parents who kick the sex talk can down the road, assuming they will learn eventually. I suspect if you brought the sex talk up to a group of adults, there would be a mixed bag of responses.

Sex Case Studies

Some of the people in the group would respond with nervous laughter. Others would respond with snappy jokes. A few of them may be crude. It can be a challenge to distinguish a group of parents from a group of giddy teens when talking about sex. We speak from our experiences, and some parents' sexual history, experiences, and training were far from ordinary, pleasant, or exportable. Here are a few illustrations from a fictional group of friends.

- Mable was molested as a child. She had lots of thoughts about sex, though mostly sad ones.
- Biff had a secret porn addiction. Most of his thoughts

were disguised behind an "I hope I'm not found out" fear.
- Marge believed men were pigs; all they wanted was sex. She shared what she thought, which was neither encouraging nor helpful.
- Bart believed sex was taboo. He had nervous thoughts when he shared.
- Mildred blushed the whole time; she couldn't wait to get home.
- Bert was crude. His perverted pleasure from the conversation contributed nothing beneficial.

Some people in the group felt as though they were talking dirty, while others felt dirty. They all had thoughts, but few of them were comfortable sharing them. The shame of Adam was all over their faces, revealing hearts that had yet to come into the practical freedom of the gospel. They were normal Christians. The people who have the most freedom to talk about sex and the clearest perspective on sex can be the most muddled and shame-ridden about sex and sexuality.

Sex and Parents

Sober talk and thoughtful discussions about sexuality are rare with Christian parents. After you compare the absurdities of the world with the maturity of God's Word, you'd expect Christians to bring bold and careful counsel to the topic of sex. Our voices should not be muted, and we should not blush. God has given us the gift of clarity and wisdom, which compels us to speak into the sexual noise of our culture, as well as speak into the minds of our children. There is no shame in a biblical worldview of sex (Genesis 2:24-25; Hebrews 13:4). Many believers do not speak with clarity, wisdom, grace, or maturity but cow down to the challenge, or they respond with silly wisecracks.

It is like we come into the discussion with a nervous apology rather than a bold vision. The result is our kids are left to figure out what sex means through other mediums than in their homes or their parents. The number one sex mentor today is social media. Parents are left behind as children find alternate means to learn about sex as they explore sexuality outside the home, among their friends. Some of these explorations are at the children's volition, while other avenues are imposed upon our children, whether they want to know about sex or not. The world does not wait for stalling and stuttering parents to lead their children. There is no inhibition from the world when it comes to teaching their version of sex education.

Sex and Maturity

Sex is not going away because God preordained sex into how we relate to each other, which is why Satan created a rival who uses perverted temptations and tactics to twist our minds (Genesis 3:6-7). Bad sex is born out of our shaping influences: what happened to us, how our parents failed to lead us, and the poor choices we have made. Our culture perpetuates our sex problems further through perversion and the intrusion of the social contagion of pornography. This social crisis should not leave the Christians covered in the culture's sexual dust. Rather than lamenting our present problems, we are called to step into our sexually dysfunctional world proactively. Sex is for the mature. Jesus came to kill and destroy the works of the devil (1 John 3:8), and He similarly armed us to go and do likewise. We don't need another statistic about how bad porn is. We need proper training that initiates a proactive plan to talk to our children about how to live a life of purity in an impure world.

Sex and Youth

The number one question people ask about the sex talk is when to have it. I have made a case throughout this book that the sexual education of our children begins before their first birthday. We began having sexual "talks" with our children before they could walk. What you don't want to do is pretend sex and sexuality do not exist, and then when they are of age for more in-depth and more complex discussions about sex, you drop a dramatic and traumatic sex bomb speech on them. That strategy does not help children or deepen your relationship with them.

A biblical worldview of sex and sexuality needs a long, slow on-ramp that incrementally leads to appropriate, unique-to-each-child discussions about the intricacies of intimacy. Each child is different; it is every parent's call to customize how they communicate the sex experience to the child. Our three children are two years apart. They are a girl, a boy, and a girl. God wonderfully and uniquely created each child. We scripted our approach to each one of them according to their individuality, gender, maturity, and unique personality traits. The only similarity is that we started having "sex communications" with them before they could walk.

Sex and Spirituality

As you can imagine, it would depend not only on whether your child is a Christian but also on the maturity of their relationship with God. Sanctification is a process, and all children move at their own pace through progressive sanctification. If your child is not a believer, they will not be able to grasp the message the way they should because they lack the Spirit's illumination and the Bible's wise guidance. Maybe you don't know if your child is a believer. That is highly possible since that kind of assessment is subjective. It is even more subjective when they are young and living under your leadership. Their true faith will be more measurable as they become adults, living on their own. If you're unsure that they are a Christian, you can still assess their overall maturity and responsiveness to the Word of God. Are they teachable? Are they open to the Lord's training? Or are they resistant?

Regardless of their spiritual temperament, the starting point for all sexual discussions is spiritual in nature because sex is a spiritual matter first and foremost. You will want to determine your child's spiritual capacity. This idea is similar to a child's ability to understand and process other things, like math. Some children understand mathematics. They get it. Other children have a harder time grasping math concepts. Your child's spirituality will be similar. At the transitional age from child to adult, girls are usually more mature than boys. You will need God's insights and wisdom as you consider your child's specific needs, strengths, weaknesses, and capacities. Regardless of age, start early. Guide the train slowly out of the station, but by all means, bring it out and get things moving. Be appropriately sexual in your speech and expressions. Let your children experience a purer version of sexuality long before they ever understand the deeper meanings of sex, especially before the culture starts indoctrinating them.

Sex and Conversation

You do not want the talk disconnected from your ongoing, transparent relationship with your spouse or children. I'm not suggesting you have inappropriate discussions before it's time for them. I'm suggesting you have a biblically appropriate, intimate, affectionate, and spiritual relationship with your spouse and child, regardless of the child's age. A child does not need to hear the talk from someone they have never cried with, sinned against, confessed to, or talked to in depth. By the time you get to the talk, you need a relational history with your child that is meaningful and spiritual. You need to be their friend as much as you need to be their parent. No matter where you are with your child, you can begin an ongoing, meaningful, and transparent relationship with them now.

If you have not had this kind of relationship with them, then you can build one by walking out repentance with them. Let them know how you have failed them and how you'd like to create a new kind of relationship with them. Humility can go a long way; God gives favor to the humble (James 4:6). Your future sex talk should be a natural progression of communication within the context of doing life together. It should not be an out-of-left-field, overly-punctuated event that freaks them out. If the talk is in the context of a life lived within a relational, familial context, and there are many appropriate talks along the way, then the actual conversation will not be awkward.

Suppose your children are older, and you have not established a relational context. In that case, I recommend you talk with your church leadership about how to reorder/restructure your home so you can serve your child more effectively when the time comes for the talk. If you are in a two-parent home, the dad needs to lead your daily conversations about life issues. He should set a pace and trajectory for sex and sexuality from a complementarian worldview. Complementarian parents build a biblical partnership, with the dad leading and the mom complementing their leadership model (Genesis 2:18). Though the mom leads the talk with a daughter, you do not detach it from her husband's leadership, care, and insights. Sex is a relationship between a husband and wife, which is a united front they want to practice in every context of their lives, especially when instructing their children about sexuality.

Sex and Language

I do not recommend parents use immature synonyms to communicate anatomical body parts. Call them what they are. Our son doesn't have a pee-pee but a penis. That's not weird to him. It is what it is. A cup is a cup, a book is a book, and his penis is a penis. Immature language or immaturity about words is not wise, and it's not helpful. You don't want to export weirdness to your children. It breeds insecurity while solidifying their shame, creating communication distance between the parent and child. Don't export your taboos, silliness, or crudeness to your children; use the right words. As your children mature, your hope is for a seamless transition to more in-depth and profound sexual discussions with them.

It's the idea of building blocks incrementally being stacked one upon another. You begin with the language, which will lead them to future drawn-out discussions about the act of marriage. Imagine spending a few days with your child, walking them through teen and adult sexuality issues, and the first two days are spent getting comfortable with a new kind of language. That's unnecessary because you can be pre-emptive. Children have an incredible capacity to understand complex things and to be mature about them if you let them. Do not be embarrassed to talk about what God was not ashamed to create and entrust to our care and stewardship.

Sex and Relationship

Let no corrupting talk come out of your mouths, but only such as is good for building up, as fits the occasion, that it may give grace to those who hear.
(Ephesians 4:29)

Sexuality discussions at a young age involve more than accurate anatomical language. Sexuality is a way of life.

While your children are young, you want to build a foundation for sex as you lavish them with affection, encouragement, and edifying communication. These concepts contextualize the anatomical aspects of sex in the framework of a loving relationship. Without them, then, your sex talk will be theoretical, sterile, and laborious. The best sex flows out of other-centered, God-saturated relationships.

Distant, harsh, neglectful, critical, impatient, and generally frustrated parents do not prepare or equip their children with a biblical understanding and experience with sex. How many women have complained about the emotional detachment of their husbands? How many women have complained about their husband's sex on the brain mentality? One lady told me she felt like a Christian prostitute because of her husband's pornographic understanding of sex. His sexual practice was all physical, not spiritual. He learned the mechanics of sex on the streets rather than from the Bible or his parents. He was not equipped to relate well to the opposite sex.

Call to Action

1. Do you have a biblically sexual relationship with your spouse?
2. What kind of sexual experience are you exporting to your children?
3. What are your children learning from your appropriate, intimate interactions with your spouse?
4. How is your home sexually characterized? Here are a few examples of a biblically sexualized home: warmth, kindness, encouragement, respect, honor, and serving. Is there anything you need to change about your home? If so, what is your plan to change?

7

Advice Before You Have the Sex Talk

The sex talk is a transitional time in a child's life, but long before you have the talk, your child will have a worldview and practice in place that will form the backdrop for how he will process what you're telling him during the sex talk. His home environment forms that worldview and develops his relational habits long before he learns about the most intimate aspects of male and female relationships.

A Sexual History

Physical intimacy is part of a relationship experience, though it is not the totality of who two people are. It is the icing on the cake, not the cake. It is the tip of the iceberg, not the iceberg. The whole cake and the iceberg are the couple's unique, full-time, uninterrupted relational adventures together. Imagine a child fed icing all his life while never given the cake. He would grow into an icing-centered adult. The sex talk isolated from an affectionate, relationship-centered home environment creates self-indulgent, self-centered, sex-centered adults. The sex talk should come in the middle of a relationship that connects a gospel-centered history with a gospel-centered future. A child does not need to hear the talk in a vacuum of technical terms that are disconnected from a God-loving relational experience with his family, as understood primarily from his parents.

Relational disconnectedness is how our culture thinks and talks about sex. They are icing-centered, myopic hedonists who are wildly ignorant of the biblical purposes and pleasures of sex. That kind of worldview and practice did not happen by accident. They came into the world with Adamic, self-centered tendencies. Their parents did a poor job redirecting their Adamic trajectories. The sex talk should be one of many talks between a parent and child within a familial culture that is God-loving and God-centered. If you have been characterized by an other-centered life, marriage, and parenting model, then your child will upload and process the talk from a biblically healthy experience. He will have biblically saturated ears to hear what you have to say because of the kind of person you have been.

Sex Is Good

Sex is wholesome and good. It is one of God's many gifts to humanity, which makes appropriate sexual discussions normal. The sex talk you're going to have with your child is probably one of the most important conversations you'll ever have with him, other than his relationship with Christ. If you are giddy about appropriate sex talk or if you have unwholesome ideas about sex, then please find help before you try to walk your child through this transitional period. You must not export an uncomfortableness about sex to him. He needs a mature and wise understanding of love, as taught from the Word of God, by secure and uninhibited parents who have worked through any dysfunctions of their pasts.

Sex should be communicated as a normal gift from God. Speak openly and honestly about sexuality to your child. Let him hear your faith in God and the goodness the Lord intends for His children through sexual relationships. Your child will learn from you. He is your student. Lead him. Speak the truth to him. Children love truth and are fully capable of embracing and responding to truth, even the deeper aspects of it. They want to be led, and their security will mature in proportion to the parameters that you use to guide them. Lead with courage, grace, and clarity. Parents need a healthy and biblical understanding of sex. If the parents are not right in their hearts and minds about sex, the children will know it, making it a challenge to communicate God's perspective to their child.

Sex, Sin, and Grace

Let marriage be held in honor among all, and let the marriage bed be undefiled, for God will judge the sexually immoral and adulterous.

(Hebrews 13:4)

Part of the talk will be negative—how some sexual practices are sinful to engage in, like sexual activity outside the marriage bed, pornography, or a gay lifestyle. You will be communicating with your child about what is right and wrong about sex, which means sexual sin is a prominent piece of the talk. For him to understand the sinful side of sex, he will need to have a right understanding of the doctrine of sin. In other words, the talk won't be the only time he hears about a good and bad way of doing things. He should already understand sin and know how to respond to sin. This perspective means you should have been teaching him about our mutual fallenness and God's redemptive measures early. The warfare between dark and light, sin and grace, should be part of your daily conversations.

One of the most effective ways to communicate your seriousness about sin and grace is through personal confession, practical application, and biblical reconciliation. Your example of openness and honesty about your failures is your most effective means of motivating him to be honest with his thoughts about sex and sexual confusion. He will upload the power of your sex talk with how you have transparently lived your life in front of your child. Your child should not hear about the dangers of sin and the gift of grace for the first time during the sex talk. He should have a healthy view of the doctrines of sin and grace by observing your sinful failures and God's grace-empowered applications in your life.

Sex and the Environment

One of the marriage goals for your child is when he is old enough to read Ephesians 5:25 for the first time that he understands the meaning of that passage. Your aim is for him to say something like, "Oh, I know what that means. That is how my dad and mom live all the time." The hope is that they will not have to be told what this text means. They will already know because of your example. Christ and the church practically lived out in your marriage is one of the most important backdrops you can give your child when it comes to having the sex talk. Imagine a dad or mom having the sex talk with their son or daughter, and their marriage has been marred and characterized by anger, criticalness, and vindictiveness. What a confusing picture of what physical intimacy between two humans is supposed to be like.

Physical intimacy born out of selfishness rather than an event that flows from the fabric of a God-centered relationship and lifestyle is not the kind of marriage training a child needs. Sex is not a stand-alone event but a lifestyle. Suppose dad and mom regularly encourage each other and regularly repent to each other. They live an ongoing restorative relationship. If so, there will be a higher than average chance their children will have a biblical understanding of sex and marriage. As you already know, it's an uphill battle. The promiscuous inclinations of our culture and what kids learn from social media make your biblio-centric example a breath of fresh air in a world that is antagonistic to the beauty, wonder, and holiness of sex. If there is holiness in the marriage, it will be easy for the child to connect sexual intimacy as a holy event sanctioned by God.

Sex and Leadership

The number one counseling problem in most marriages is the passive male. The fall of man and the indoctrination of our egalitarian, feministic culture have nearly fully emasculated the male to the point where he does not want to lead his family—or he's afraid to lead. He is not encouraged to lead his family. He is not expected to lead his family. He is not trained to lead his family. And women are more than willing to take over. The Bible assumes biblical male leadership from the husband. If the husband is leading properly, he will provide a beautiful marital picture of Christ and the church that will bring biblical clarity to a child who lives in a sexually dysfunctional universe.

It is less challenging for a boy to learn how to lead sexually when his dad is the leader in the home. No offense intended here, but a wife cannot teach a boy how to be a man. That's like a cow trying to teach a bull how to be a bull. It takes one bull to know another one. The husband must lead his wife through the process of preparing for the talk with their child, whether the child is male or female. It takes two different people—male and female—to engage in biblical sex, and it takes a male and female to prepare to engage their children in the sex talk.

The husband models leadership, the same leadership he wants his son to exhibit as a husband. The daughter also learns from her dad what biblical leadership looks like in the home as he leads his wife. The daughter experiences biblical headship through his example. There is no better template for a boy or girl to learn what biblical leadership is like than from their father. Dad, do not delegate the preparation for the sex talk to your wife. You both play an integral part in preparing your child for a biblical understanding of sexuality. Do it together. When the boy is old enough to marry, he will have a wonderful template for biblical masculinity. The dad's leadership will also be invaluable when it comes time for his daughter to marry.

Sex and the Culture

The culture will not slow down and wait for you to get your sexual life and message together for your child. Don't lament how things are. Expect it while being proactive in communicating your life and message to your child. Your intentionality will put you out in front of your children as you turn their hearts and minds toward biblical things while slowing down cultural encroachments. The world will run over you and your child. Show your child a better way. Your example is that way (Ephesians 5:1; 1 Corinthians 11:1; Philippians 4:9). If your example is radically different from the culture's sex message, then it will be easy for your child to discern right from wrong. If your language, attitude, lifestyle, insight, wisdom, and habits are only marginally different from what our culture offers, then when it comes time to have the sex talk with your child, the information you offer will be murky, confusing, and possibly lost on them. Be proactive, alert, diligent, sensible, mature, and biblical about sex and sexuality.

In the last chapter, I discussed some of the basics for having a sex talk with your child—an overview of sorts. I hoped that many new parents would read it and begin thinking about how to talk to each other and their children. It will come sooner than you think, and rigorous biblical groundwork is essential. In this chapter, I have provided more details about what your home life should be. I hope to expand parents' thinking. The talk is not just about sex but about a life lived before God, their spouse, and their child. You could classify these two chapters as parental preparation for the sex talk. They form the backdrop for having the actual sex talk with your child. In the next chapter, I will discuss some practical pointers for going on your retreat with your child and introduce some core materials that will help you navigate this transitional time in the life of your family.

Call to Action

As you have read this foundational content, you may have realized your home is not as God-centered as it needs to be. Maybe you perceived how the sex talk loses some of the biblical force it needs because of an inconsistent walk with God. If that is the case, then may I suggest two things:

1. Failure in the family dynamic does not mean you're disqualified from walking your child through the sex talk. You can repent of your failures and receive God's and your child's forgiveness. Repentance can reconcile your past and change your future.
2. As you walk out repentance, prepare to take your child through this crucial season in their life.
   If these ideas are new or overwhelming to you, then find someone in your church who can come alongside you.

8

Instructions for the Sex Talk

One of the most exciting and bittersweet times in a parent's life is walking their child through the sex talk. It's the season that leads them into adulthood. It's the secret handshake that lets them know that the curtain of childhood is dropping and a brave new world is in front of them. It's exciting because you are the one leading them. It's bittersweet because your little kid is growing up.

Exporting Jesus

The previous chapters of this book laid out a strong gospel-centered backdrop that prepares a parent for the sex talk. This foundational training incrementally built a sexual worldview in the child's life from birth to the sex talk. As you know, the talk is not just a talk. It's a way of living out a God-centered and other-centered perspective. You're exporting your sexual worldview and experience to your child, which makes your goal much broader than teaching abstinence. Any middle school health class can do that for you. What you're exporting is the life of Jesus Christ—the gospel—to your child, specifically how that life impacts their sexuality. The previous chapters represent a practical philosophy for gospel-centered sexuality. This chapter is about the actual talk—the weeks before as you prepare and the days you spend with your child discussing the birds and the bees. More than likely, this will be the most emotional time in your child's life.

Six Months Out

The gospel implies preparation (Ephesians 1:3-11). You want to be intentional during this season. The gospel was not a haphazard event (Galatians 4:4) cobbled together because of an unexpected failure of humanity. God thought about us in eternity past and mapped out a specific and practical strategy to help us. As practical modelers of the gospel, you want to imitate Him by being proactive in your preparation for launching your child into adulthood (Ephesians 5:1). Few plans you will ever make are more important than preparing your child for this time in their life. One of the things you want them to feel is your thoughtful care as your well-planned sex talk engages them. Important events are planned events. The Lord plans, prepares, and executes redemptive initiatives for His glory and our benefit. Six months out should be sufficient time to begin putting the materials together for your retreat.

What I'm going to lay out here is what we did. This chapter should be filed under the heading of "a" way versus "the" way of doing things. Knowing the difference is wisdom. Because the Bible is not clear on how to execute the sex talk with your child, you should exercise purposeful freedom to do what you believe is the right thing for you (Romans 14:23). What we did may work for you; it may not. Choose parts of what we did and add your preferences. In one sense, it does not matter how you do it as long as you are leading your child into adulthood through the means of a practical gospel-centered worldview on sex and sexuality. Your child's personality, spirituality, capacity, and maturity will determine a big part of your plans. Your talk should be predetermined and pneumatic (Spirit-led). If you have more than one child, you already know a cookie-cutter parenting model does not work.

Talk Time

Knowing each child is different will help you decide when to have the talk with them. We talked with our daughter two months before her eleventh birthday. There were several reasons for this.

- Her body was changing, and we knew her first period was not far away.
- It was late summer, just before school started, which allowed Lucia time to take her on a four-day retreat.
- She was going to middle school, and we assumed the language and lifestyles in her new school environment would be a significant cultural upgrade.
- She was well-grounded in God's Word and was mature enough to where we believed she could handle this transitional conversation in her life.

There is no set age for the talk. You'll have to assess your child, their surroundings, peers, contexts, and spiritual maturity. The timing was right for us and her. We waited until our son was between twelve and thirteen years old.

- His body was not changing.
- He was not entering a culturally upgraded school environment for another six months.
- He was not interested in girls.
- He was interested in rip-sticking, tree climbing, and Minecraft.

Talk Materials

Around the six-month mark, we began gathering materials for the talk with our daughter. Six months gave us enough time to read and listen to the materials so we could assess them. We assessed the materials' strengths and weaknesses and considered how they should be applied to our child. We listened, read, and made notes with our daughter in mind, which helped Lucia as she prepared for the talk. If you are a single parent, I recommend you work through the material with another adult who knows you and your child. The gospel is not only proactive in planning but also customized to each person. God's Word is not a generic Word but a specific Word that speaks to specific people. Therefore, we wanted to adapt the materials to a specific little girl–our little girl.

The main core material we used was from Family Life– their *Passport to Purity Kit*. This program was adequate, with some tweaks, for what we needed to do. Lucia and I listened to all the CDs separately, making notes and comparing their strengths and weaknesses, as well as discussing how to apply the lessons to our child. *(They may have changed the materials since we used them between 2012 and 2016)*. In addition, we used an article from CCEF, written by Paul Tripp, called, *The Way of the Wise: Teaching Teenagers About Sex*. While *Passport to Purity* is excellent on the technical aspects of the talk—e.g., how to have sex, body issues, your period, virginity, and planning the actual retreat—it had some weaknesses. Here are three of them:

- They do not use much Scripture. You will want to make sure your child has a good grasp of the Word of God. Family Life could assume this essential biblical grounding.
- There were some man-centered aspects to the program. For example, if you want to overcome

peer pressure, they focus on you mustering up the courage. They don't speak clearly enough to our innate weaknesses or our need to rely on God rather than ourselves (2 Corinthians 1:8-9).

- The thrust of their curriculum was more about not having sex or getting pregnant. While this perspective is a good and needed goal, there needs to be more emphasis on the motive for purity, which is Godward, not pragmatic.

Talk Prep

They were trying to do two main things: how to prepare for the talk and how to talk. On these points, they excel. You will not be disappointed. You may preview the Travel Journal for the parents for the purity retreat and the Tour Guide from Passport to Purity. If you want a more Godward focus, you will have to add your preferred teaching to your plans. While we didn't want our child to have sex before marriage, the more important key is how she rivets her heart to God rather than the shame of fornication or the liabilities of having a child outside of marriage. We also added the Alex and Brett Harris book, Do Hard Things. This was not a book we used on the retreat. We gave it to our daughter just before the retreat to read, which she began. She finished it after the retreat. There were two reasons we gave her this book:

- We wanted to heighten her awareness and anticipation for the upcoming retreat. Though she did not know the specifics of the retreat, she knew she was going to something special—we built it up.
- We framed it as a time for her to be with her mommy and talk about the next phase of her life. We did not tell her about the sexual aspects of the retreat, as that would have confused her.

She was ecstatic about the adventure, and giving her a book about being a teenager heightened her anticipation. Though she loved Nancy Drew mysteries and other girly-type books, we wanted to add "Do Hard Things" to her reading list. She embraced this idea as she was looking forward to being an adult. The last piece of material we used was the location for the retreat. We picked the mountains of North Carolina, which were about 90 minutes away. Our daughter and mother love God's creation. The mountains were the perfect place for them to romp around the woods, walk in the creeks, and slide down big rocks. We wanted it to be fun because we knew there would be embarrassing and fearful moments during the talks. She needed to go romp in the creeks after hearing where babies come from. I took our son to the beach.

Two Months Out

With your location determined and your materials in hand, it's time to start working through them. If you live in a two-parent home, I recommend both parents read and listen to the material. You can plan some date nights for discussion. Because my wife was going to have the talk with our daughter during the late summer, we used several Vacation Bible School nights to go on dates to discuss the materials. This time gave us opportunities to talk about the strengths and weaknesses of the materials as well as the strengths and weaknesses of our daughter so we could practicalize the one to the other. These times were also opportunities to pray through the plans. These date nights proved to be rich, not only because they were related to our daughter but also because they strengthened our relationship.

The Retreat

We had some friends who owned a house in the mountains, and they were willing to let Lucia and our daughter use it. Because there was no school, we planned a four-day retreat. They left on a Monday morning and returned late Thursday afternoon. The Passport series does a good job of laying out the plan for the retreat. You can actually do it over a weekend, but because we could add an extra day, it was great as it gave them more time for additional discussion points:

- We wanted to carefully unpack her relationship with Christ, which the Passport series does not do.
- We wanted to learn how we could parent her and her siblings more effectively. It was a wonderful time for us to learn how to be better parents.
- Lucia planned all the meals and snacks and bought all those items prior to the retreat.
- She also went online to research the area to see what fun things they could do while there. This was an important aspect of the trip.
- She knew parts of the talk would be heavy and embarrassing for our daughter, which it was. There were a couple of times when they needed to stop the audio and discussion to climb some rocks, which made a huge difference.
- She also planned downtime for our daughter so she could work through her passport journal. She took her journal writing so seriously that she wrote everything on paper beforehand and then rewrote it in her special passport journal. She didn't want to mess up her special journal for her special occasion.
- Another heavy moment was the all-important trip to the drug store to buy feminine products, which also required another trip to the rocks and creek. She

handled all these things extremely well, and I was praising God that she had a capable mom to walk with her every step of the way.

Lucia's faith in God grew during this time. Her affection for her daughter grew deeper, too. The bond between them was strengthened, and we all celebrated God's kindness to us (Isaiah 55:8-9).

Post Talk Events

On the way home from the retreat, Lucia planned a time at the salon for both of them to get their hair styled and get manicures and pedicures. It was a great way to cap off her time with Mommy. Later that evening, I met with them for a prearranged dinner, during which I had the opportunity to encourage our daughter as we celebrated this transitional week in her life. I gave her a promise ring and walked her through our hope that she would glorify God not only in her body but also in her heart (Luke 10:27). It turned out to be four full days of celebratory seriousness and fun. Though she was back playing in the woods and acting silly again, we knew things would never be the same. Our little girl walked across the bridge from being a girl to becoming a young lady. It was the beginning of a new adventure with her.

Call to Action

1. If your child is a toddler, I recommend you read through this book now. If you are married, it would be best for you and your spouse to read through it together. Though the sex talk may be years away, your child's sexual worldview is developing now.

2. If you are a single parent, I recommend you talk with someone in your local church to discuss the ideas in this book. You do not have to go through this alone.

3. Perhaps you have put off the sex talk until the last minute. That does not have to be a problem. For many of us, the sex talk was put off permanently. If you're like me, you learned about sex and sexuality as an adult after you became a Christian. There is much grace for people like us, and if you're in my boat, you can appropriate that same grace into your life.

4. Even if you're a last-minute parent, I recommend you begin at the beginning of this book. You may not be able to implement some of the teachings into your child's life, but you can adjust and shape your thoughts by these truths, so when you do have the talk with your child, it won't be from a blank slate.

About the Author

Rick Thomas launched the Life Over Coffee global training network in 2008 to bring hope and help for you and others by creating resources that spark conversations for transformation. His primary responsibilities are resource creation and leadership development, which he does through speaking, writing, podcasting, and educating. In 1990 he earned a BA in Theology and, in 1991, a BS in Education. In 1993, he received his ordination into Christian ministry, and in 2000, he graduated with an MA in Counseling from The Master's University. In 2006, he was recognized as a Fellow of the Association of Certified Biblical Counselors (ACBC).

Other Books Available from
Life Over Coffee

Boasting in Weakness
Centering Your Marriage on Christ
Communication
Complete Marriage
Don't Apologize
Exchange the Truth for a Lie
Help My Marriage Has Grown Cold
Identity Crisis
Local Church
Loving Me
Mad
Marriage Devotion We Are One
Politics and Culture
Parenting Devotion from Zero to Adulthood
Sex, Temptation, and Modesty
Storm Hurler
The Cyber Effect
The Talk
Wives Leading
You Decide